SO YOU'RE TAKING UP GOLF?

BY THE SAME AUTHOR

QUIET ON THE TEE

KILL IT BEFORE IT MOVES

WHAT IT IS, IS GOLF

TEACHER WORE A PARACHUTE

SO YOU'RE TAKING UP GOLF?

BY JOE JAMES

Illustrations By the Author

South Brunswick
New York: A. S. BARNES AND COMPANY
London: THOMAS YOSELOFF LTD

Library of Congress Catalogue Card Number: 68–27232

A. S. Barnes and Co., Inc.
Cranbury, New Jersey 08512

Thomas Yoseloff Ltd
108 New Bond Street
London W. 1, England

6549
Printed in the United States of America

CONTENTS

SO YOU'RE TAKING UP GOLF?

1

SO YOU'RE TAKING UP GOLF?

IF YOU HAVE NEVER PICKED UP A GOLF CLUB BEFORE THIS moment, it is not too late to back out. Do it now—quick—while you can get away with it gracefully. Once you have formally taken up the game, quitting is virtually impossible. You cannot announce "I quit" or "I retire from the game." Your pride will require a convincing alibi, like a collapsed lung or a broken back. Anything short of that and your golfing buddies will know you chickened out.

So before you join the ranks of us golfers, think it over carefully. Weigh the consequences gravely, for golf will hook you as surely as heroin.

If you haven't already taken your first lunge at the ball, if your lips are still unsullied by unprintables, hold off until you read this epic tome. Let me tell you of the woes, the frustration, the elation, and the despair that lies in wait if you take up this crazy game called golf. Then, if you still feel you and golf belong together, head for the first tee.

2

MISERY IS THE TIE THAT BINDS

LET'S START WITH THE REALLY IMPORTANT THINGS YOU should know about golf. Nothing so elementary as how to putt, or swing, or which club to use or how to fade or hook a shot. You will pick these up easily enough. You must delve deeper into the game and the players. Investigate as carefully as you would inspect an insane asylum before having yourself committed. Study the swingers inside!

And be prepared to suffer! Suffering and intense anguish are the very soul of the game. Golfers suffer from the moment they tee off until they putt out on the eighteenth hole. But it is a delightful suffering which brings them back again and again. This suffering, or common misery, is the cement that holds every foursome together.

Make a random check wherever golfers assemble and you will find that the guys who cannot break 100 play together. So do the guys who shoot in the 90's. The 80-shooters play with their own kind, and so do the low handicappers. They do not join together in these foursomes week after week because they share a common degree of skill. They play together because they share a common degree of suffering.

Suffering, or common misery, is the cement that holds every foursome together.

The golfer who cannot break 100 is in constant mental anguish for that reason. He begins each round confident that today he can do it. He has it within his grasp—at least while on the first tee and addressing the ball. From then on "breaking a hundred" slips away in a continuing chain of frustrating hacks, chops, and shanks. He plays with other guys who cannot break 100 because he gets comfort from their similar frustration. When he misses a shot, he knows one of the other golfers will also miss a shot and very soon. When the goof comes, relief surges over him. And so it goes for eighteen holes: frustration, relief; frustration, relief.

But, you ask, what about the scratch golfer, the guy who plays a perfect or near-perfect game. Ah, my friend, he suffers worst of all. He plays with golfers of equal minimum awkwardness, men who make each shot with machine-like precision. When this scratch golfer finally messes up a shot, his frustration is appalling and his suffering is beyond all comprehension. For him relief does not come quickly. His par-shooting companions may go on hole after hole, executing each shot perfectly, never three-putting a single green. An hour may pass before one of his companions goofs. His is the supreme misery. Relief is never seconds away.

Golf courses are designed to amplify these frustrations and miseries. Tennis courts have backstops to intercept a missed shot and send it bouncing back to you. Bowling alleys never penalize you for a goof. Instead, mechanical devices snatch up missed pins before people get a chance to laugh at your clumsiness and send the ball hurrying back so you can try again. But a golf course is fiendishly designed to pounce on you the moment you goof and gleefully rub salt in your wounds. This is a fact of life, something you must accept right along with separate tees for the ladies. Every golf course is designed to lie in wait for your first goof and then compound it. If you submit meekly and take a penalty stroke to get your ball back in play, the course will let you stumble on. After all, you

A golf course is fiendishly designed to pounce on you the moment you goof and gleefully rub salt in your wounds.

have admitted the course has you whipped. But suppose you refuse to give in and take a penalty stroke. Suppose you choose to stubbornly play the ball out of a grove of towering trees, for example. The trees, incensed at your audacity, rise up to smack the ball back in your face. Then the course sadistically slams you with not one but two extra strokes and maybe more.

Frustration is there by design. If you have progressed far enough to hit the ball straight, the designers bend the fairways right or left in what they call dog-legs. This term is derived from the expression, "Let's treat the golfers like dogs!" If you learn to hook or fade the ball with the fairway's curve, the designers stick in traps at strategic intervals to lie in wait and swallow your ball.

Golf courses are designed to entice you, much like a Venus Fly Trap. The place where you tee off is elevated and the grass is cut nice and short. To make the first shot even easier on each hole, you are allowed to place your ball on a little wooden pedestal so you cannot miss it. This is the subtle come-on, the lure to get you off the tee and out into frustration. All of these conveniences are yours at a place where you need them least. But let your ball stray out into the rough, into tall and wiry grass, and the rules suddenly change. Now, when you could use some help, you are not permitted to put the ball on a wooden pedestal. Now you cannot even touch it before you swing at it. You must play it, or at least try to play it, where it lies, and lies, and lies.

True, some golfers shrug off this planned frustration and charge merrily ahead. One who had driven his ball into the deep rough quickly inserted a tee in the tall grass, put his ball on it, and sent a shot screaming back into the fairway. At the risk of losing a few teeth, I asked this stranger, "Do you always tee up your ball in the rough?"

"I only tee it up in the rough when I have a fur piece to go!"

"Nope, not always," he grinned, as he dropped his driver back into the bag. "I only tee it up when I have a fur piece to go!"

More than likely you, like millions of other golfers, will insist on conforming to the rules. If you do, be prepared for frustration—frustration that pulses through the game like blood through your arteries. Be prepared to accept the growing harassment that follows each shot short of perfection. Know that just because you play the game *longer* may not necessarily mean you get *better*. Our threesome of long-time hackers invited a lone golfer to join us. He quickly pointed out that he had taken up the game just two weeks earlier. As we left the first tee, I remarked to one of my buddies that the novice's drive was well beyond his. "And that guy," I reminded him, "has only been playing golf two weeks!"

"So what?" my friend growled. "Wait until he's been playing *four* weeks!"

He had a point there. This newcomer was still unaware of the frustration that hovers over every fairway and laps up against every cup. He was hurrying along dumb and happy. When he does become aware of this lurking misery he will be like the rest of us—apprehensive, and frustrated. Then, and only then, will he begin to fully enjoy the strange bittersweet game called golf. Then, in rhythmic phases of apprehension, misery, and delight he will play golf again and again. Like the little boy who kept butting his head against the wall, he will play golf because it feels so good when he stops.

LINES TO A GOLFER WHO CAN SMILE NO MATTER WHAT HAPPENS

Show me a man who can smile
 When his drive dribbles into a ditch.
Show me a man who can laugh
 When he's flubbed a simple pitch.

Show me a man who can chuckle
 After missing the shortest of putts.

Show me this man, find him if you can,
And I'll show you a guy who is *nuts!*

3

THE DRIVING RANGE: A TENDER TRAP

THE DRIVING RANGE IS THE VERY CORNERSTONE OF GOLF. It is the Pied Piper that lures happy, contented armchair loafers and television watchers from the comfort of their homes and into the game of golf. Yet the pundits who write about the game spend all their time telling you what to do on the golf course with never a mention of driving ranges.

The driving range is a cunningly contrived trap. It attracts innocent non-golfers the way bright lights attract moths. Each tee is a tiny stage upon which the complete novice may strut and prance. An ever-present gallery of spectators, folks who don't know a duck hook from a swan, is there to watch and marvel at the shots that slice out into the darkness.

Once you've been lured into the driving range by the bright lights and the action, once you take your place on the rubber mat and swing at your first ball, you are astounded at the simplicity of the game. You lunge and the club smacks the ball and sends it soaring like a rocket past the 200-yard marker. You tee up another ball and

Each tee at the driving range is a tiny stage upon which the complete novice may strut and prance.

sock it and away it goes. Everything you do looks great. Shots that go high bounce almost as high again. Low shots zip like a bullet and still reach the 200-yard marker. There is really nothing to it.

If the guy on the next tee is having trouble, you saunter over and help him. When you get him straightened out, you walk serenely back to your private stage, tee up another ball, and smack it into the night. This game is so simple it's no wonder guys like Palmer and Player and Nicklaus do so well at it week after week.

At about this point it occurs to you that the real game of golf is not here on the driving range but out on a course waiting for you to conquer it. If you can do this well at a driving range the golf course should be duck soup. So you buy clubs and shoes and get ready to take up the game. You are hooked, trapped by a recruiting

The wide expanse of driving range is gone, suddenly squeezed down to a narrow fairway crowded by tall weeds and towering trees.

device that keeps right on snaring more golfers for waiting golf courses. Blissfully ignorant of what has happened to you, you head for the golf course. Then the Honeymoon is suddenly over.

There is no rubber mat on the first tee. Instead, you stand on soft turf that gives when you swing. The stiff rubber tee is gone. Now the ball rests on a fragile wooden tee. Even the ball has changed. The range ball with the wide red stripe that made it so easy to see is gone. Now the ball is a little white blob teetering on the tee. The wide expanse of driving range is gone, suddenly squeezed down to a narrow fairway crowded by tall weeds and towering trees. At the driving range the ball used to bound along like a rabbit. Here it hits the soft turf and stumbles to a stop. At the driving range a bucket of balls was a mere arm's length away. If you missed a shot, you forgot it and teed up another ball. Out here the ball is an Albatross chained to your neck. If you slice it into the woods, you must go after it. You cannot tee up another ball and ignore the one out there. You are the ball's slave and you must follow wherever it leads you, hacking away in growing frustration until you finally get it into the hole. Then, on the next hole, the agony starts all over again.

The swing that had become fairly smooth back at the driving range now falls apart. The ball becomes a frustrating little white devil, something you must pursue and hack at in growing desperation. You could quit. You could walk away and leave the ball lying there in the weeds. But this has been done only once before in the annals of golf. The fellow who did it was a young lieutenant named Arnold. The fact that he quit in the middle of a game dogged him for life. In fact, it ruined Benedict's career. So you must keep at it, and the eighteenth hole finally arrives. You head sadly for your car, a mere mortal again. But you do not sell your clubs or give your golf shoes to your brother-in-law. You are hooked. Your first sane thought is to get back to that driving range and work on your problems.

Back at the driving range, the endless buckets of balls are waiting and the individual mats beckon in the warm arc lights. You take your place in the chorus line but now, perhaps, you begin to notice things you didn't see before. The range-owned golf clubs, the ones you used before to make those tremendous drives, have wider faces than conventional clubs. You realize too that the rubber mat supports you solidly: the big red stripe around the ball makes it easy to see and hit. The ground out front is hard and dry. Balls roll and roll and roll. There are no fairway borders to brazenly remind you that you have sliced or duck hooked. The 100-yard marker is invariably 75-yards out, the 150-yard marker is 110, and the 250-yard marker is a scant 180 yards from your rubber mat. Any ball that gets off the tee looks like a great shot.

You realize now that the driving range is the come-on that got you hooked on golf. Without driving ranges to lure new recruits, golf courses would have faded away like jousting courses long ago. You are hooked, and there is little you can do about it. For you it will be an endless cycle–from golf course to driving range and back to the golf course. You are now one of legions in endless pursuit of perfection.

Since you will be coming back to the driving range with regularity, much as a hypochondriac goes to the doctor, you may as well enjoy it and the people out there with you. Remember that many are complete novices still in Stage 1. They have not yet moved to the Stage 2 bit where you buy the clubs and shoes and take up the game. That comes later. So move in among them with confidence. Ignore the driving range's woods in their inviting racks. Instead, bring your own clubs. On one visit, take only irons. Tell the guy behind the counter, so all nearby can hear, that you came out just to work on your irons. Word will flash along spectator row. "There's a real, genuine golfer. He came out to work on his irons. He looks like somebody I seen on TV." Other hackers, lunging with drivers and striving for distance, will pause to watch you pass. You move fluidly down the chorus line, relaxed and confident, casually practice-swinging several irons with a gentle, fluid motion. Pass on down the line to the turf. Shun the rubber mats as you would the plague. Take plenty of time to warm up. From their little stages, the hackers will watch you covertly. Many have never seen anyone hit a golf ball off grass before.

Do not worry about how well you hit the shots. Concentrate on getting the ball off the grass. If you get the ball into the air, few onlookers or other novices notice if it has been hooked or sliced. They sneer only when you whiff, missing the ball completely. So slap the ball and never leave it sitting there on the grass. Always finish with arms extended and high. Finish each swing with serene confidence as you gaze far out into the darkness.

You can expect some of the beginners to come over and see why you do so well. For this reason, start off with a five iron or six iron. When the kibitzer comes over, mutter, "This nine iron is getting 'em out pretty good tonight!" If he asks for advice, give it in abundance. After all, you have been on a real golf course.

But always be prepared for the unexpected at a driving range. A stranger may walk up and say, "Pardon me, but I've been watching you and I think I know what you are doing wrong." Turn slowly and fix him with an icy stare. Pull yourself to your full height, choose your words carefully and ask, "May I see your handicap card?" That alone may be enough to send him on his way. But if he does happen to know what a handicap card is, he will ask, "Why do you want to see my handicap card?" Come right back with, "I'm a 4-handicapper myself. If you're a 3-handicapper or better, I'll be glad to let you show me what I'm doing wrong. Otherwise thanks, but no thanks!"

If you tire of this fun with onlookers, you might even decide to work on improving your game. Some golfers do this at driving ranges. They tee up a ball and say to themselves, "I'm on the number five tee. It's a par four, slight bend to the left," and whack the ball. If the drive is good, they muse, "Okay, that leaves me an eight iron to the green and the green is off to the left, just behind that hundred-yard marker." Then they hit the eight iron. If it misses the target they say, "Well, left myself a thirty yard pitch." They then select a nine iron or seven iron and pitch the ball at an appropriate marker. A few fellows find this such fun, minus all the frustrations of a bona-fide round of golf, that they never go near a real golf course again!

4

THE SWING IS A SIMPLE THING

THE GOLF SWING IS A SIMPLE THING. THEREFORE SIMPLE people make the best golfers.

Hitting a golf ball with a club is no more complicated than hitting a nail with a hammer. If you have ever missed a nail and hit your thumb, you will recall this happened because you did not keep your attention entirely on the nail. Your fertile and creative mind was moving along to things far more important than the nail head. So it is with hitting a golf ball. People of broad intellect take in other aspects of the game, or of life, while they are swinging. If their alert and inquisitive mind does happen to dwell on hitting the ball it also, in a flash, takes in other aspects of the swing—matters like the arc of the backswing, the point at which the weight shift begins, clubhead acceleration on the downswing, and rate of rise after the ball is hit. They let their minds soar. Because of this, the ball usually doesn't.

On the contrary, people with simple uncomplicated minds see only the golf ball resting on the turf. They miss the broader aspects of the game, the philosophical impli-

People with simple uncomplicated minds see only the golf ball resting on the tee or turf. Therefore simple people make the best golfers.

cations and the creative challenges. They have their hands full with the problem of just hitting the ball. Therefore they hit it better and more often.

Proof of this is everywhere. Think for a moment of the great minds in history. How many great thinkers or creative geniuses were great golfers? Einstein was not a golfer. He probably tried the game but gave it up because his mind flashed far beyond the simple problem of hitting a ball with a club. Chances are Winston Churchill shanked a few shots and turned his spare time activity to painting, where his imagination could soar as he wielded the brush. Euclid, Dante, Shakespeare, Disraeli, Ben Franklin, and Thomas Jefferson were not low handicap golfers.

So if you play poorly it should merely emphasize the fact that you have a broad intellect and quick comprehension for important details. You are not a simple type.

If you want to play golf, and play it well, you must develop the ability to be a simple thinker. When you step out on the golf course, you must turn off your soaring imagination and inquisitive creative mind as you would turn off a faucet. For eighteen holes, become a slow-thinking golfer with a one-track mind. You will not think

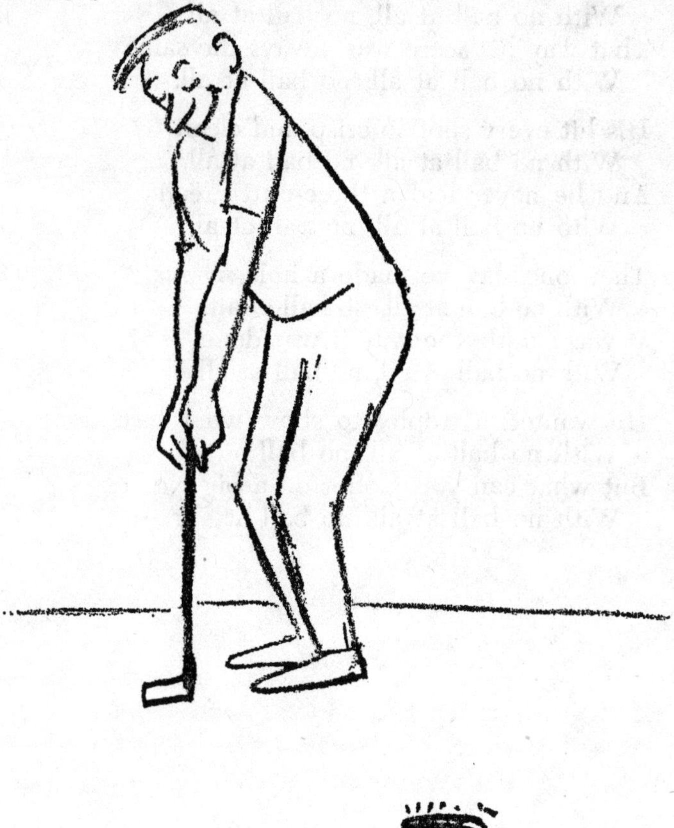

of a new way to cut plant production costs, but you will clobber the thinking men in your foursome.

The secret of playing good golf is simple: If your game is stinking, quit thinking.

THE GOLFER WHO PLAYED GOLF WITH NO BALL AT ALL

There was a golfer who played the game
With no ball at all, no ball at all.
That way his score was always the same
With no ball at all, no ball at all.

His hit every shot so crisp and clean
With no ball at all, no ball at all.
And he never had a three-putt green
With no ball at all, no ball at all.

Then one day he made a hole in one,
With no ball at all, no ball at all.
It was simple the way it was done,
With no ball at all, no ball at all.

He wanted a trophy to show what he'd done,
With no ball at all, no ball at all.
But what can you mount on a big No. 1,
With no ball at all, no ball at all?

5

FINDING GOLF COURSES AND GOLFERS

PROBABLY THE MOST IMPORTANT THING YOU NEED TO KNOW before you play your first round of golf is the correct address. This is not how to stand over the ball. That can come later. You need to know the address of the course.

Do not snicker. More time is lost every week trying to find the golf course than is ever lost in factory coffee breaks. Golf courses are hard to find. And some won't let you play after you find them. These are the exclusive ones where you have to be the son of a long line of sons to enjoy membership. It is too late for you to do anything about that.

Once you find a golf course where you are permitted to play, your next problem is finding someone to play with. No one likes to play golf alone. Misery likes company. Without someone along to keep you honest, the game is amazingly simple and not much fun.

Golfers you approach will ask how well you play. They need this information to be sure they won't lose bets. They usually ask politely, "What is your handicap?" Answer: "I lie a lot."

The quickest way to get an invitation to join a threesome is to flash a roll of bills and a fast backswing in that order.

Handicapping got its name because it restricts or handicaps the golfer, making it more difficult for him to rinky-do or con the other golfers. Golfers are often accused of padding their scores so their handicaps will be higher. Then they would be in position to sand bag a stranger. This is rarely the case. Most golfers are jealously proud of low handicaps. An 8-handicapper wants to be a 7-handicapper. It galls him to put down a score that will boost his handicap. Many just don't put the score down at all or they chop off strokes. They do this even though a higher handicap would help them win more bets, or at least keep from losing money. Instead, they "handicap" themselves by putting down a *lower* score than they actually shot.

"They had us three down, but then I threw a string of double bogies at 'em and closed 'em out!"

Knowing all this, you should not be awed when a stranger tells you he is an "8-handicapper." Take the strokes he gives you, a 24-handicapper, knowing the odds are in your favor that he'll shoot a 90 instead of an 80. He might even shoot 100. If he does shoot 100, he'll tell you earnestly that he's way off his game. Nod sympathetically as you take his money.

When you join strangers for a round of golf, their main concern will be in setting up the bets. Such matters as "greenies" and double for birdies will be discussed. No one will mention fundamentals like whether or not you will improve in the rough. Once the match starts, it is too late to discover you are not all playing the same game. I joined a three-some recently and we played six-hole robins. That meant we would change partners after each six holes. On the 10th hole, I noticed one fellow in our group was carefully and covertly teeing up his ball on a clump of grass every time he got out into the rough. I started to call his attention to this then and there. But suddenly I realized he would shortly be my partner. So I decided to keep quiet and profit, if possible, from his cheating. After all, it was my turn.

"Say, ol' buddy, is it too late to press?"

Sometimes you wonder if the fun and stimulation derived from "robins" and "skins" and other forms of friendly betting is really worth all the preliminary maneuvering and post mortem computing. When you're the big loser, the others surround you the way cannibals close in on a captured missionary. They compute *your* losses with fiendish satisfaction. But when *you* win, one wise guy will ask, "How'd we come out on the bets?" And a loser will say, "Aw, it's late. And besides, I don't want your money. Let's skip the bets."

Some golfers love to bet, but hate to lose. It is not the small amount of money involved, but the stigma of losing, of paying off in plain sight of other golfers. A stranger joined our foursome. We prepared to tee off with our usual private bets working but this guy suggested a robin. We suggested two-bit robins. (Twenty-five cents bet on each six holes.) He upped it to a half-dollar. When his team was down, he was the first to yell "Press!" And when the game was over our new friend was obviously the big loser. As we headed for the nineteenth hole he said, "I'll put my clubs in the car and join you."

We were busily computing this guy's losses when someone exclaimed, "Say, where is that guy?" One of our group raced to the parking lot, just in time to see our late buddy whip his car out of a parking hole and head for the open road. Our man raced in front of the car, with reckless abandon, and flagged him down. "You owe us $2.50," he told the startled driver. "You lost three robins and two presses."

So if you bet and win, remember Houdini wasn't the only guy who knew how to disappear into thin air. Stick with your pigeon like a leech until you get your money. If you are a frequent loser, it is wise not to park on the parking lot. They always look there first.

Golfers tend to be click-ish. They do not like to have a newcomer shoved into their group by the Pro shop. For this reason the Pro usually acts as an agent, not telling you who he plans to have you join until he has approached the threesome with the opening. They can then secretly size you up from afar. The Pro is anxious to get as many players as possible on the course and keep them moving. He prefers one foursome to a threesome and a onesome. The threesome is deathly afraid they will draw a rank beginner. This is not because they worry about having a rank beginner join them. Having a clumsy golfer in your foursome relieves your own frustration. What you do not want is a clumsy golfer who never knows where his ball stopped rolling. This golfer will look up, miss his shot, stare after it for a split-second, and then tell everyone what he did wrong. Meanwhile his ball is bouncing off into the high grass. He has no idea where his ball finally came to rest. So he begins hunting

A bank president may covertly tee up his ball in the rough to win a fifty cent bet.

for it. The others are expected to help. This happens time and again. So when a threesome sizes you up as a prospective fourth, they are not concerned about

how well you play. They are trying to determine whether you are a ball-watcher or a lip-flapper.

You may prefer to find your own threesome rather than have the Pro introduce you. The quickest way is to flash a roll of bills and a fast backswing, in that order.

When you join a threesome, there is no sure way to tell what kind of group you are joining. Some say you can tell an honest golfer by the size of his ears or the width between his eyes. Others say a man's status in life will more or less mark him for you. Nothing is farther from the truth. A bank president may covertly tee up his ball in the rough to win a fifty-cent bet. A minister who just finished a rousing sermon on fair play and moral integrity may "accidentally" drop the flag while you're putting. On the other hand, a full-time burglar on his day off may be the most honest golfer you'll ever meet.

6

GAMING THE PLAYERS

THE NEWCOMER TO GOLF THINKS THE PURPOSE OF THE GAME is to shoot a low score. This is not true at all. The goal of any golfer is to win bets. It is not how you play the game, but how you game the players.

First, let's talk about gaming your irons. There are two types of iron shots. The first is the Ego Shot. You use the Ego on par three's, usually where there is water or some other hazard between you and the green. Even if you are not first up, yank a club from your bag and announce, "This looks like a seven-iron to me! And that might be too much!" Always announce an iron which you know will never clear the hazard. Any sane person would know it too, but not golfers. The others in your foursome will also yank seven-irons out of their bags even though it is obviously a five-iron shot. And chances are one who has been out-driving you consistently all day will give you a disdainful half-sneer and announce he's hitting an eight-iron. After the three have plopped into the water, you can go ahead and hit the four-iron you planned to hit all the time.

The other iron shot you need in your repertoire is the

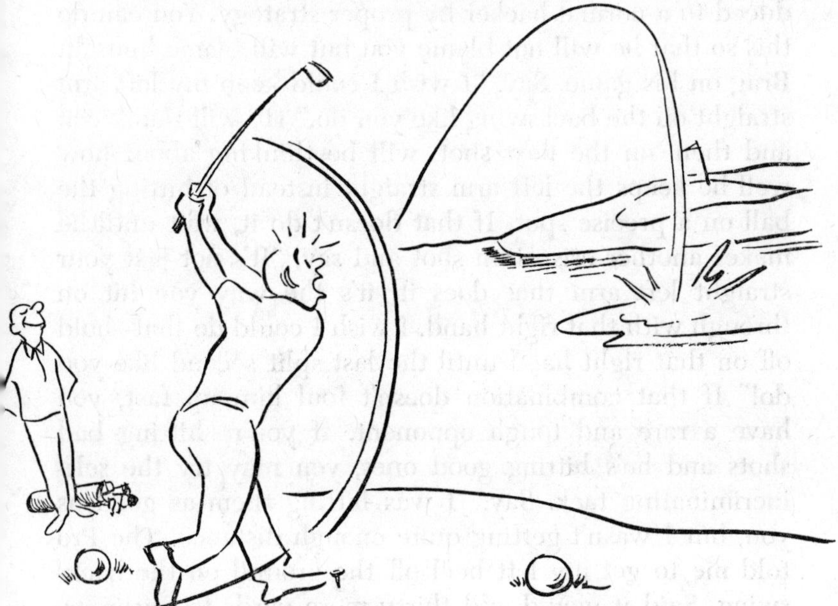

After the three have plopped into the water with seven irons, go ahead and hit the four iron you planned to hit all the time.

delayed trap shot. It is used *after* you have made any iron shot. One of the players will invariably ask, "What club did you hit?" If you hit a four-iron and made the green, tell him you hit a six. A six-iron will put him in one of the sand traps in front of the green. All of us need practice getting out of sand traps. If there is water or a trap behind the green, tell him you hit a two-iron. You can compound the confusion if, just as your friend is on his backswing, you claim, "Oh, I'm sorry. What I hit was a five-iron!"

Any opponent who is playing irons well can be reduced to a normal hacker by proper strategy. You can do this so that he will not blame you but will blame himself. Brag on his game. Say, "I wish I could keep my left arm straight on the backswing like you do." He will thank you and then, on the next shot, will be thinking about how well he keeps the left arm straight instead of hitting the ball on a precise spot. If that doesn't do it, wait until he makes another crisp iron shot and say, "It's not just your straight left arm that does it, it's the way you hit on through with that right hand. I wish I could do that—hold off on that right hand until the last split second like you do!" If that combination doesn't foul him up fast, you have a rare and tough opponent. If you're hitting bad shots and he's hitting good ones, you may try the self-incriminating tack. Say, "I was hitting them as good as you, but I wasn't getting quite enough distance. The Pro told me to get my left heel off the ground on the back-swing. Said it would add thirty more yards to my irons. But I just can't remember to get it up." No matter how well your buddy is hitting his irons, he secretly wants to hit them even better and farther. So he will try the left heel bit, secretly—of course—and you will have him in your pocket.

Remember always that advice can torpedo any golfer but it must never be obvious that you are giving it. The golfer who openly "instructs" others in his foursome will suddenly be playing by himself. Instruction must be so subtle and indirect that no one can catch you at it. The results are just as devastating. Every golfer's Achilles heel is a deep motivating desire to play better. The golfer who gets a par secretly wishes it were a birdie. The guy who gets a birdie secretly wishes it could have been a hole-in-one. For this reason, all golfers are vulnerable.

The guy who clips you by repeatedly chipping up close to the pin is not immune. Brag on his consistency; then plant the seed of discontent. "I played with a guy last week who was deadly around the green just like you." Your opponent will beam. Then snap the trap: "You chip 'em up and let 'em roll. Terrific! But this guy opened the face of his nine-iron more. Called it a cut shot. The ball flew higher, but when it hit, man, it stopped cold!"

Let that soak in and, at the next opportunity, your opponent will try the cut shot. He'll flub it, secretly cussing himself for trying such a fool shot when he had the pitch and roll going so well. On the next hole, he'll go back to the pitch and roll approach. But it won't be

The Frog Hair Finesse is a handy weapon for sabotaging opponents on the putting green.

there anymore. The touch he had will be gone. Then he, too, is in your pocket.

There is an old saying, "You drive for show and putt for dough." So let's talk about putts. Not yours, but other people's putts. Winning at golf calls for more than just sinking your own putts. It calls for an ability to make other people miss putts. This form of sabotage around the greens must, like instruction, never be an obvious thing. That would be unsportsmanlike. If you stoop to such crudity as talking when the other guy is putting or dropping your putter or offering outright advice you will be quickly ostracized. So let's talk briefly about the more subtle skills around the green like the Frog Hair Finesse and planting the Three Putt Phobia.

Use the Frog Hair Finesse when you're farthest from the pin and have to putt first. Hit your putt carefully, then step back and watch it roll. If your ball goes close to the hole, and the green is fast, say "Wow! This green is slow. I really banged it!" If you failed to get close to the hole on your approach putt, the Frog Hair Finesse is again the *wrong* reason. If the green is slow, say, "I knew it was fast, but then I froze and barely hit it!" Then stand politely aside while your opponents also fail to reach the "gimme" range.

The Frog Hair Finesse can actually be a part of the other golfing skill, planting the Three Putt Phobia. It may be Stage 1. Planting the Three Putt refers primarily to a situation where you are already close to the pin and your opponent has the long putt and must go first. Here you are expected to refrain from any advice and stand quietly by until your opponent has made his long approach putt. By that time it may be too late. So take quick and direct action to set up a Three Putt. Start it as you walk toward the green. Say, "Your putter is really hot today. I don't believe you've had a single three-putt green, have you?" That sets him up for his first one. If he has had several three-putt greens, he is even more vulnerable for the Three Putt Planter. Just remark, "Here's another of those long approach putts. They sure have bugged you today! But don't let this one get you. Put her right up there next to the pin! You can do it!" Or, while your opponent is lining up his putt on a lightning fast green, remark softly but quite distinctly to your caddy, "This green isn't going to fool me. It looks fast, but it's gonna take a good firm putt to get there!" Your opponent will hear you and indecision will move in. He will be torn between hitting the putt gently, as he originally planned, or smacking it firmly. He will do neither—and be a cinch for three putts and maybe four. Indecision, deftly planted, blooms in seconds.

Even after you have exhausted the Frog Hair Finesse and the Three Putt Phobia all is not lost. You can still resort to the Short Putt Putrifier, a technique for spoiling other people's short putts. If you're putting first and your straight-in putt drops, exclaim, "Well I'll be darned. Made it anyway, but I sure didn't see that break when I lined it up!" If a break really exists close to the hole say, "That's the kind I like, straight in!" If you miss an easy straight-in putt and your opponent is waiting to try one just like it exclaim, "I didn't see that break, I flat didn't see that lousy break!" Even if your opponent cannot see a break, he will worry about it. His putt will putrify.

As the match draws to a close, you may find all your ammunition is exhausted. If your opponent has a short putt left to beat you, re-use of the Short Putt Putrifier may be out of the question. You must now use different strategy. Announce, "I haven't got a chance. You're deadly with that putter today. I think I'll give it to you. No, I

Nobody else can read a green like George can!

won't do that. But putt it, and put me out of my misery!" All this chatter, while most gracious, completely derails your opponent's concentration. Then be politely quiet while he misses the putt.

Never tell an opponent he cannot make a putt. All golfers rise to a challenge. Remove the challenge, and a putrid putt is in the offing.

Putting is a matter of concentration. With a little practice, you can develop many little bits of business that will get your opponent's mind off his putt and on other things. For instance, drop useful hints while lining up your putt. "I didn't know," you might announce, "that in the morning the grass bends toward the sun!" Or, on a green near a water hazard, exclaim "Well, doggone! I've always heard grass near water bends toward the water. But this is the first time I've ever been able to see it!" The other guys won't be able to see it either, but they'll be thinking about it—right up until they miss their putt.

7

PLAYING YOUR OPPONENT'S WOODS

COMMAND OF THE WOODS IS JUST AS IMPORTANT AS COMMAND of irons. Good control of the driver, for example, means getting off to the right start on each hole. Good control of fairway woods can be the difference on a par 5 or long par 4. By control of woods, of course, we mean how you control your *opponent's* woods

You can learn to control your own woods well with practice. The difference in any game will always be how well you can influence the other guy's woods. Here again, as with the irons and putting, the action you put on his wood game must be as subtle as a lizard's breath but as deadly as a cobra.

You begin using your wood game well before the group tees up on No. 1. The time to turn it on is just as soon as you meet your opponent or opponents. There are several schools of thought on this pre-tee activity. The Whammy school favors direct affrontery, but with the prescribed subtle touch. The exponents of the Florida Fizzle favor a more genteel system based on polite suggestion. Both systems can be devastating.

The "Welcome" Whammy is started the moment you

shake hands with your opponent. Size him up openly and show genuine admiration at what you see. "This guy looks like he can knock it a mile off the tee," you exclaim as you uncork the Whammy. "Look at those wrists and forearms. Man, if I had arms like that I could lay it out there 275 yards!" If the guy is small, then the Whammy goes, "Say, you've got a build a lot like Gary Player. Same big forearms and supple movements. I bet you can knock those woods a mile!"

That's all you say. You want to leave one thought uppermost in each guy's mind. If you say anything else, or even start a conversation with one of the other players, the Whammy is diluted and may even fail completely. Remember that hitting a driver, especially off the very first tee, requires concentration. If you managed to get your Whammy across, your opponent will start his backswing thinking about the nice things you said. Half-way through the swing, his mind will go blank. He will suddenly realize he has to hit the ball, will lunge at it and may even miss it completely. As he stands there mumbling and watching his ball roll fifty yards off the tee, say "Aw, that's too bad! But those things happen." Then tee up your own ball and bust it. Do it knowing your Whammy execution was superb.

The Fizzle is executed differently. It also begins the moment you meet your opponents. Say, "I sure hope my game is better today. I've been having trouble slicing. Any of you fellows bothered with a slice?" Chances are they'll mutter an emphatic "No" and try and change the subject. But go right ahead with, "The Pro told me to move my hand around under the shaft like this but it hasn't helped. And this first tee is rough on slices. It's out of bounds on the right, ain't it?"

I told you he hits a long ball.

If you feel talk about a slice is too elemental with veteran golfers, change the slant. "I've been skying a lot of shots," you might begin, "and this time last week you guys woulda' had me in your pocket. But the Pro told me how to stop it. He had me keep the club head on the ground as I started my backswing. It really works! I'm ready for you guys today!"

Say nothing more. As your opponent starts his backswing, he will be thinking about your remark. He may even peek at his backswing to be sure he keeps the club head on the ground as he takes it back. He won't sky the shot. But he will top it.

The Ego shot you used works well on the woods too.

"See that bush out there on the right—the one about 275 yards down the fairway? Well, this little guy put his ball past that bush!"

It is especially good if you win the toss and tee off before your opponents. After you hit your drive, watch it roll and say, "See that bush out there on the right—the one about 275 yards down the fairway. Well, I played with a guy last week—a little fellow—who really whipped that club head through. Took it back fast and sorta' threw his body into the shot at the last second. Well, he put his ball *past* that little bush! And just a little guy!" Then step politely aside, say nothing more, and let your opponents hit their shots. Each will be thinking about that little bush instead of hitting the ball. Each will think, "Take it back fast and throw that body in at the last second." Each will forget one minor detail; to watch the ball. Your round will be off to a delightful start.

Never waste the Whammy or Fizzle in a match where "Mulligans" are given on the first tee. A "Mulligan" is an extra tee shot granted in case you flub your first drive. At Jewish country clubs it is often called a "Goldberg." So use the Whammy or Fizzle only when it counts.

Fairway woods can be handled in about the same way. As you walk down the fairway, you might say, "I played with a guy last week who shanked wood shots! I'd never seen anybody shank wood shots before. Seen lotsa' irons shanked, but never woods. Have you ever seen anybody shank a wood?" That should do it.

There are numerous variations of the Whammy, Fizzle, and Ego shots. You can create many of your own with just a little thought. Work on this portion of the game. It will pay great dividends.

8

FITS, BUT NOT FITNESS

IF YOU'RE TAKING UP GOLF TO "KEEP IN SHAPE," TO LOSE weight, or for any of a score of other "fitness" reasons, don't kid yourself. The game will give you fits, but it won't keep you fit.

The guy who tells you he plays golf to keep in shape is usually shapeless. He rides a self-propelled cart. After nine holes, he runs the cart right up to the nineteenth hole door to get a cold beer before taking off on number ten. If he could drive the cart inside the clubhouse to get his beer he would do it. During a round of golf he drives the cart as close to the ball as possible. Many clubs post warning signs to keep golfers from driving carts right up on the green. The first offense draws a warning, the second draws a month's probation with loss of cart privileges and the third offense gets the member kicked out of the club. Usually any golfers you see walking are on probation.

Riding in a golf cart is a poor excuse for exercise. About all the exercise you get comes from climbing out of the cart and then climbing back in and sitting down. You will build up a few muscles, but these are all con-

If you plan to ride in a cart, tumbling lessons are a good idea.

nected with sitting down. The exceptions would be the right gastrocnemius muscle which does benefit slightly from depressing and releasing the accelerator and the left tibialis anterior muscle, which is exercised by picking up the left foot to apply the brake.

So if you do decide to ride carts, do it because you want to rest while you play golf and are too pooped to walk. Admit this, and enjoy the ride. But a word of caution before you climb into a cart. Treat all golf carts exactly as you would a strange cow pony. Treat them with respect. The best way to get on a golf cart is from the left side. This way you get to be the driver. If some one else is going to drive, try and observe him with other passengers before you consent to ride with him. You might readily get into an automobile with him and whizz along the freeway. Riding a golf cart is something else

If he could drive his cart inside the club house to get his beer, he'd do it!

again. Watch him closely to see if he veers to miss tee markers or petunia beds. Pick a golf cart driver who stubbornly runs over sprinklers and through gopher holes. Select one who charges through broken bottles without veering. This is the safest kind. He will never swerve suddenly to miss a daffodil and throw you out, shattering your elbow or worse.

If you are the driver, be sure your liability insurance is in force. This is even more important than coverage on your car. You need plenty of personal liability coverage, comprehensive collision, fire, and theft. Yes, theft.

Suppose someone steals the cart you rented while you are four-putting a big green? Or suppose your passenger has his wallet lifted by other than the legal method? Comprehensive collision? Two carts collided on a bridge and one went over the side; it dropped into a fifteen-foot-deep creek. They were lady drivers, but that doesn't mean it couldn't happen to you. Liability coverage? A dentist swerved to miss a squirrel and tossed out his passenger, who was also a dentist. Broke his right elbow and this dentist happened to be right handed. The result? A friendly suit and a settlement in the ten thousand dollar neighborhood. Which, by the way, is not an exclusive neighborhood. So if you plan to drive a cart, get the coverage before the cart.

Some golfers use caddies and say they do it so they can walk and get exercise. Walking four miles in four hours means you average a mile an hour. Whoever worked up a sweat at that clip? About the only sweat walking golfers work up is when they are two down on a press with two holes to go. They do get some mental exercise by planning shots and reasoning which way a putt will break. But eventually they start asking the caddy to do this for them too.

If you decide to use a caddy, admit you're doing it because you like to have the caddy around for advice. But remember that you become an employer when you hire a caddy and this brings up an entire series of employer and employee relations. We won't go into all the ramifications here; you can consult your labor relations attorney on this. Just realize that the caddy has certain rights. The rule about no more than fourteen clubs, for example, was initiated by the caddy lobby. So was the one about not looking for a lost ball for more than five minutes. Most local rules about slow play were also caddy inspired. Caddies like to get home at a reasonable hour. During one long and arduous round, a caddy followed his employer into one sand trap and then the next, into woods, ditches, and gullys. Finally he took something from his vest pocket and studied it intently. "Don't worry about the time," his employer snapped, between lunges at the ball, "you'll be well paid!"

"This ain't no watch," his caddy replied. "This is a compass. We're *lost!*"

You may as well level with caddies and let them know you are a novice at the game. They will find it out anyway. One newcomer to golf tried to masquerade as a long-time golfer but his caddy wasn't fooled. After hacking around in the rough the golfer finally got close enough to see the green in the distance. He deliberated before selecting a club and then haughtily asked, "What do I need to get home from here?" The caddy was not impressed. "I don't know," he replied. "Where do you live?"

A few golfers pull hand carts. They do not do this, in most cases, for exercise. They do it to save money. Some do pull carts for other reasons. They pull them because they consider it sissy to ride or because they do not want to get involved in personnel problems created by hiring caddies. These guys who pull hand carts are invariably men who work outdoors—postmen, Pro football players, and air hammer operators. Already hard as nails, they are the only golfers who should relax by riding in carts.

So we've made our point. Whether you ride or walk, golf won't keep you fit.

Now let's kick another fallacy in the teeth. Golf *will*

not help you relax. This may sound like blasphemy, but it is true. The business about golf helping you relax is another Old Golfer's Tale concocted to ease consciences about sneaking off from work or neglecting important week-end chores. It is true that golf will help you forget all the tensions of your job or home life. But golf will provide tensions of its own to stretch your nerves like banjo strings.

Tensions create illnesses. This is a basic medical fact known by all of us who have studied medicine by watching the medic shows on TV. Since golf reeks with tensions, it is logical that the game has spawned its own category of illnesses. One of the most prevalent is "Slicer's stomach," where the sufferer breaks out in a cold sweat and throws up clubs. "Cart Rider's Coronary" often strikes the older golfers. This type of coronary is brought on by unexpected physical anguish or extreme anger, often when the golfer discovers all available carts have been rented. Other common ailments that plague golfers are "Hacker's Hernia," "Hooker's Hypertension," and the "Look Up Ulcer." Golfers who frequently stiffen or shake when putting suffer from "Putter's Paralysis," which often goes into a secondary stage called the "Yellow Yips." Acute paralysis of the larynx or voice box occurs often and is more commonly called "Loser's Laryngitis." The slower-playing golfers, who take more than the normal four hours to navigate the course, frequently suffer from "Country Club Kidney."

There are many more ailments that can be acquired on a golf course. We have just touched on some of the more common ones. We won't even attempt, in this limited space, to cover the various mental problems golf can create. It is in this area of human suffering that all of the frustrations and anxieties really get in their licks. If you want to pursue this on your own, and you really should do this if you take the game seriously, consult any qualified psychiatrist. Do this on any day but Thursday. That's the day they all play golf.

By now you can see you are only kidding yourself if you take up golf to keep fit. Admit you are taking it up to have a good time or to get out of work or out of the house for a few hours. If tension is already bugging you, take up croquet. Sending a tension-plagued man out to take up golf is like throwing a drowning man an anvil.

You will soon be the healthiest golfer on the course. You will also be the loneliest.

If you have no other way to keep fit—no park to run in, no place to do push-ups, and no weights to juggle—there is *one* way to get lots of exercise playing golf. Share a cart with a buddy and let him drive. Put your clubs on the cart and trot alongside. Better still, after each shot let him get well out ahead with the cart and then lope down the fairway to catch up about the time he reaches your ball. You will perspire freely, you will stay in great shape, but your companions will shun you like one of those characters in a deodorant commercial. You will soon be the healthiest golfer on the course. You will also be the loneliest. Golf, after all, is a Gentleman's game. Don't louse it up by sweating.

9

THE GAME MUST GO ON

BY NOW YOU REALIZE THAT A GOLF COURSE IS NOT ALL sweetness and light, not all bliss and happiness. Pain and suffering are no strangers to the fairways, or the rough either for that matter. Now that you know about Slicer's Stomach, Country Club Kidney, and the other ailments that plague golfers you know the men who seem to stride happily along are frequently in misery. But such is their courage and such is their fortitude that they never quit until the ball is holed out on the final hole. "Finish it" is the unwritten code of the game. Even when a member of a foursome collapses, the others carry on and do not desert him. Despite their dedication to the game, golfers are human beings. They take a stricken member with them, never leaving him to expire alone on the course. If their route passes near the club house, he is dropped off with loving care near the Pro shop. This is especially true if he owes several bets and, in his condition, is physically unable to open his wallet and settle up.

A foursome of elderly golfers played together every Saturday. On one morning, Senile Sam was the first member of the foursome to tee off. He addressed the ball and then, before he could hit it, keeled over.

His three friends moved briskly along, ever thoughtful of their pallid buddy in the golf cart.

Luckily one of the golfers was a doctor. He examined Sam and announced, "Sam has suffered a stroke!"

Under the doctor's skilled direction, they lifted Sam into a golf cart and made him as comfortable as possible. "You understand, Sam," the doctor explained, "that you cannot play golf again—at least not this morning."

Sam, gasping for breath, nodded silently beneath a damp towel. "You also understand," the doctor continued, "that if we take you back to the club house we'll lose our place and won't get another tee-off time until long after noon?" Again Sam nodded, his face a dull grey. "That would be out of the question," he whispered. "I must wait for proper medical attention."

So the threesome moved off down the fairway with Sam slumped in a cart. From time to time, a member of the foursome thoughtfully poured a little cool water on Sam's ashen brow. If the foursome behind was not pressing, the doctor also checked Sam's pulse now and then. Whenever they passed near other golfers, the doctor always got their attention and yelled, "Wonder if by chance you fellows might have some oxygen?" Nobody was carrying oxygen, so the three golfers played on. Sam was quieter now. His gasps were fainter and no longer disturbed the putting.

It was most unfortunate that the course was not laid out so that the ninth hole finished near the club house. As it was, Sam had to ride through the full eighteen-hole round. But his three friends moved briskly along, ever thoughtful of their pallid buddy in the golf cart. They finished the round, settled all bets, and then the doctor rushed over to call an ambulance.

Gently, lovingly, they placed Sam in the ambulance. Then, like true friends, they climbed in with him for the race to the hospital with siren screaming.

"Will I make it?" Sam asked faintly.

"I think so," the doctor replied.

"Well, I'm sure sorry about the round," Sam murmured. "I really messed it up."

"Not at all, not at all," the doctor exclaimed. "Sam, that was probably the best round you'll ever play—if you live. You set a *new course record!*"

"I did?" Sam gasped.

"You sure did," the doctor told him. "Sam, you're the first man to ever go eighteen holes with just *one* stroke!"

The magnitude of it was slow in seeping through to Sam's weakened senses. When it did, his eyes brightened and he gasped, "One stroke! That's great, just great!" And then, with a faint smile on his lips, he added, "I just couldn't do much better than that, now could I, Doc?"

The doctor pursed his lips in thought. "Well, I wasn't going to say anything, Sam," he said slowly, "but I did notice there on the first tee that you had your right hand on top too much. Now if you'd move it under the shaft just a little more . . ."

10

GOLF, A DISEASE OF THE BLOOD

BEFORE YOU MOVE OUT ON THE FIRST TEE TO TEST YOUR new-found knowledge, please remember what you're letting yourself in for. Golf will take you over exactly like one of those body-snatching creatures in a space fiction thriller. It will permeate all your waking moments. You will be like the man whose wife berated him at breakfast with, "All you ever think about is golf, golf, golf."

"Aw Sweetie," he countered. "You know that's not so. Pass the putter, please."

No one who takes up the game is ever the same again. The changes in personality are so subtle you're never aware of them. Your best friend can take up golf and you'll be blind to the gradual change in his thinking and his work. If he's an architect you may miss it completely when he talks about a building that "dog legs." If he's a doctor, he's liable to ask his nurse for a nine-iron when what he really wants is a number 3 scalpel. That's the way golf affects people. Just thinking about this makes you wonder what would have happened, for example, if Bill Shakespeare had been a golfer. Some of his best-

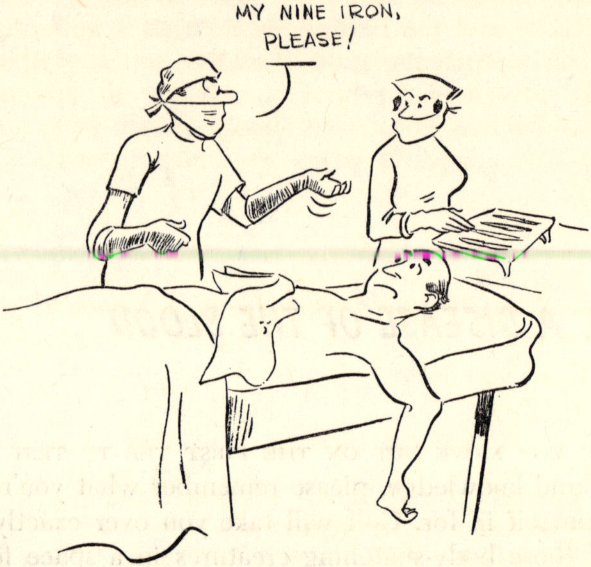

No one who takes up the game of golf is ever the same again.

known lines would be remembered far differently. Bill's putting might have inspired him to write instead, "All the world is a putting green where each of us waits on the frog hair for his turn and then flits and cavorts for his moment on the green, lines up his putt, misses it, and staggers on to the next tee."

If Shakespeare had been a golfer, he would have been plagued with a slice like most of us. And working to correct it, he might have written his soliloquy for Hamlet about like this:

> To slice, or not to slice—that is the question. Whether 'tis nobler in the mind to suffer the slings and arrows of outrageous fortune or take arms against a sea of troubles and, by changing my grip, end them. To hook,

to slice no more, and by a hook to say we end the heartache and the natural shocks that a golfer is heir to. 'Tis a consummation devoutly to be wished, to hook, not slice. To hook, perchance to dream. Ay, there's the rub! For in that change of grip what screams must give us pause when we come up with a duck hook!

School children who recite the immortal lines of Longfellow might well be memorizing poetry with an entirely different slant if Henry Wadsworth had been a hacker. For if Henry had been a golfer, his "Village Blacksmith" might have been written like this:

THE VILLAGE GOLFER

Beneath the spreading chestnut tree
The Irate Golfer stands.
He eyes the ball and bile and gall
Go pulsing through his glands.

The Village Golfer, a mighty man is he
With broad and sinewy grip
But the big clown can't keep his dead down
And there's another "Chili Dip."

See how he bends his club around the tree
With a strong and solid whack
He bends other clubs in powerful hands
You can hear the steel shafts crack.

See how the irons crumple in his grasp.
They'll never be the same.
And the Village Golfer, with an angry gasp
Has given up the game!

Even poems about more gentler subjects would have changed tremendously if their creators had been golfers. Joyce Kilmer's "Trees" might well have become "Putts":

I think that I shall never see
A putt that rolls just right for me.
A putt that breaks from left to right
That curves and then drops out of sight.
A putt that takes off straight and true
When I forget to follow through.
A putt that's never short or wide
A putt that shuns the amateur side.

Poems are written by any nut
It takes real talent to sink a putt!

It's easy to see how golf can infect the finest works of writers and artists. Even statesmen are not immune. We cannot tell what golf is doing to present-day politicians. That will be a matter for historians. But we can well imagine how, for example, an addiction for golf might have affected Abraham Lincoln.

"Honest Abe's" reputation for truthfulness would have handicapped him a great deal. A true golfer does not mind bending the truth a bit where his score is involved. Lying about your score is acceptable. But it is a downright sin to get caught at it.

Abe's rail-splitter swing would have given him a fast backswing. His beard would have been a putting handicap. So the chances are that Abe would have been a hacker like the rest of us. And instead of his famous address, written on the back of an envelope, he might have written the following on the back of a score card after nine holes:

"Four score and seven strokes ago, I stood on the first tee, dedicated to the proposition that all golfers are created equal. Now we are engaged in a one-sided match testing whether this golfer, or any golfer with my horrible slice, can long endure.

"Four score and seven strokes ago, I stood on the first tee . . ."

"The world will little know or long remember what we scored here because when we get to the clubhouse I will throw away the score card. It is altogether fitting and proper that we should do this."

That's about the way Abe would have written it *if* he had been a golfer. So if you take up golf, be prepared for the game to color almost anything you do. But it will be a pleasing color.

11

WATCH OUT FOR THE CLODS

GOLF IS A GENTLEMAN'S GAME, BUT NOT ALL GOLFERS ARE gentlemen. A few are Clods.

A Clod is a slob with golf cleats. Sooner or later, if you pursue the game of golf, you will cross trails with a Clod or even find one of them in your foursome. So it is high time you know how to recognize Clods. This requires a little study because there are several strains of Clod and also because you cannot always recognize a Clod by his appearance. A distinguished professor may be a Clod in disguise and the guy who took up the collection at church last Sunday may be a ring-leader among the Clods.

One of the most prevalent strains is the Big-Footed Clod. You recognize this type by action around the green. The Big-Footed Clod does not pick up his feet as he walks. He drags them, shuffling along so that his spiked feet slash the green like a vegetable grate. The Big Foot cleans mud off his shoes while standing on the green. He does this because it is obviously the best place to stand and not get more mud on shoes while cleaning mud off. The Big Foot will also range right up to the cup,

A Clod is a slob with golf cleats.

tramping close to it when there is no reason at all. This makes a ridge around the cup and may even cause the Big Foot to miss a putt. When a Big-Footed Clod misses a putt, he stomps his feet and twists them angrily into the green. A raw slash of earth in an otherwise velvety green is a sure trail sign that a Big-Footed Clod has passed this way.

Another abundant breed is the Care-Less Clod. These

clods are not clumsy. Often they are skilled and well-coordinated golfers. It's just that they couldn't care less. These Clods yank the flag from the hole and throw it carelessly aside, whacking a foot-long dent in the green. They slap the pin back in just as carelessly, often nicking the sharp edge of the hole. When your cinch putt rolls right to the lip and then veers suddenly, a Care-Less Clod has been there first. You can also tell one by the way he marks his ball. The Care Less Clod does not use a coin. He uses a tee and scratches a criss-cross mark on the green. This is quicker and simpler, but the criss-cross may be the reason your long putt suddenly swerves off course just enough to miss the hole.

Sand Clods inhabit the traps. Their ranging habits are easily predictable. A Sand Clod enters all traps from the high side, sinking knee deep in the soft sand. He hacks at his ball until it is out of the trap, then leaves in the same general direction he entered. He has no fear of pursuit and leaves his tracks and slash marks for all to see. By noon on many golf courses, sand traps look like a swarm of kids have been playing in them. It was really a school of Sand Clods. Many golfers are embarrassed for others to know that Sand Clods frequent their course. They use rakes or golf clubs to smooth the traps and hide the tell-tale trail of the Sand Clods. This helps for a little while, until another school of Clods comes through.

These strains of Clods are bad enough, but every now and then you will run across the acme of Clods. This is one who embodies all the traits of the Big-Footed Clod, the Care-Less Clod, and the Sand Clod—and then some. This is the Complete Clod. The Complete Clod ranges over the entire course, not just around the greens and traps.

When you think you have located a lost ball and hurry over to find a crumpled cigarette package, you've stumbled on the spoor of the Complete Clod. This strain of Clod strews ball wrappers, candy wrappers, cigarette packages, matchbooks, beer cans and bottles along the course like a garbage truck with the bottom knocked out. He may even smash a bottle now and then with a nine iron, just to test his swing.

The Complete Clod never repairs a ball mark on the green. It would only take him seconds, using a tee, to pry up the cavity and then press it gently level with his foot. Each brown spot on the green, where grass has died over-night in an unrepaired mark, tells you the Complete Clod has been this way. He also leaves burning cigarettes and even cigars on the greens. Sometime you may mistake them for worm dropping, but the seared grass around

Never attempt to defend yourself with a golf club.

the residue should help you identify the mark of the Complete Clod.

A walking Complete Clod is bad enough, but whenever one gets loose in a golf cart the course is really in big trouble. These mobilized Complete Clods run the carts right up on the green apron and sometimes even get a wheel on the green itself. They drive the cart on the tees, often leaving themselves barely enough room to swing without hitting the cart.

Remember these strains of Clods and their characteristics. Do this and you will never lapse into becoming one yourself. Many Clods just don't care, but a few are merely ignorant. These ignorant ones can be saved and often become delightful people to have in your foursome.

When you do find a Clod in your foursome, or see one tearing up a green or trap, be extremely careful. Let one of the older and bigger golfers tell him about the way Gentlemen play this game of golf. A Clod, when provoked, can be dangerous. This is especially true during mating season. Clods are quick-tempered. Instead of knocking your teeth out with his fist, a Complete Clod may come at you swinging a club like a broadsword. Do not attempt to defend yourself with a golf club. You may parry an overhand smash, but the other shaft will break when it hits yours. The club head will keep coming and a surgeon may shortly be stitching up your scalp, or worse.

If you are attacked by a Complete Clod, fight him with your golf bag. Throw it down and run.

Frog Hair Flub

12

WHAT ABOUT THE WEATHER?

WE REALLY SHOULD SAY A FEW WORDS ABOUT WEATHER, but not many.

Most golfers do not admit that weather exists. They develop a closed mind. You can tell one, "Ol' buddy, we cannot play today. It is raining, which occasionally turns to sleet. The wind is blowing up to forty-five miles an hour in gusts. If we play today we will catch pneumonia, or worse!" Your friend will say, "My mind is made up, don't confuse me with no facts." Then he'll flip a coin into the icy blast and you'd better call it quick if you want a chance to tee off first.

That slogan the post office people have about "neither rain, nor hail, nor snow shall stay them from their appointed rounds" may well have been lifted from a Pro shop wall.

So there really isn't much to tell you about golf and weather, except that the weather is out there. And if you're a golfer, you're in it.

LINES TO A THOUGHTFUL GOLFER

When a thoughtful golfer writes his will,
  He remembers each golfing friend
And specifies burial any day,
  Except on a sunny week end!

13

GOLFING AND THE GREAT BEYOND

THERE'S A SAYING THAT OLD GOLFERS NEVER DIE, THEY JUST hit every shot with a wood.

Golf is a game you can play as long as you are among the living. Once you take it up, chances are you can keep right on playing it until the Great Scorer asks you to slip the covers on your earthly clubs for the last time and move on up to that Golf Course in the Sky.

Surely they must have a golf course up there. No avid golfer can imagine the Great Beyond without a golf course. Any Paradise without a golf course would, if you'll pardon the expression, be Hell.

So let's assume that all good golfers, in the moral sense, go to that great Golf Course in the Sky. But what happens to the others, the Clods who fail to make the cut and must join the Pro Below?

THAT GOLF COURSE DOWN BELOW

The life I lived was pretty bad,
  And when it came time to go,
St. Peter slammed that Pearly Gate
  And motioned me down below.

I begged him to please let me in
  The tears welled up in my eye,
"All my life I've dreamed," I told him
  "Of that Golf Course in the Sky."

Good golfers go to that Golf Course in the sky. Clods who fail to make the cut must join the Pro below.

He slammed the bolt home hard and firm
  "You can play down there, I know,
Just tell Satan you're a golfer,
  And ask where to find the Pro."

I wandered through hot steaming mists
And found someone who could tell
Where I should go to find the Pro
Of the golf course here in Hell.

"Just through the sulphur pits, my friend
And ignore the stinkin' smell.
You'll find the Pro who'll let you play
On our golf course here in Hell."

The Pro was a hulking devil
Hairy and covered with soot.
His eyes glowed like livid coals
That sizzled under each foot.

He handed me a set of clubs.
The handles were glowing hot.
"A guy who plays down here," he said,
"Will remember every shot!

"Our tees, you see, are glowing coals
That sizzle, and pop, and crack.
Each tee's a hundred yards in length
And the marker's at the back!

"The fairways are steaming cauldrons
Where smoke billows up belly high.
We never touch the ball down here
Each shot is a sizzling lie!

"You have used liquid center balls.
Now move your game up a peg.
Down here in Hell, my golfing friend,
Each ball is a rotten egg!

"The grass towers out in the rough
In massive and slimy brakes.
When your ball goes in there you find
It's not grass but cobra snakes!

"The fairways are steaming cauldrons where smoke billows up belly high. . ."

"The greens are fiery red down here.
  The flag's on a red hot pole.
You can putt on one green all day,
  For you'll never find a hole!

"Drinking fountains stand everywhere,
  Lemonade squirts cold and pink.
But each fountain fades in a flash,
  When you start to take a drink!

"You're always behind an eightsome.
It takes days to play one hole.
We have no sand in traps down here,
Each is filled with burning coal!

"You must follow the burning ball
Through smoke, fire and burning pit.
Here you play the game forever
The Pro will never let you quit!

You who still live and play the game,
Won't you shed a tear for me.
Staggering o'er this fiery course
From now to Eternity!

Do not cheat in the game of life,
Keep your score card pure and clear.
Be good up there, my friend, because
It's sure Hell to play down here!

Ah, but there is a brighter side! Among the millions who play golf there are many who never fudge when they mark their balls, who never tee up balls in the rough, and who never forget strokes. There are many who fix ball marks and replace all divots, many whose lives are as pure and fine as a shot to the pin. When these clean-living guys play their last eighteen and turn in their clubs for the Grim Reaper to store, they head for that wonderful Golf Course in the Sky!

If you take up the game there'll come a day when you too will knock on the Pearly Gate and ask for the Head Pro. Old St. Pete will take a long and thoughtful look at the handicap sheet he's been keeping on you all these years. Then he will either suggest that you catch the first bus for the course down below or he will swing wide the Pearly Gates, fit you with a Heavenly set of matched clubs, and point the way to the first tee.

And what will it be like on that Golf Course in the Sky? Well, just listen:

THAT GOLF COURSE IN THE SKY

The old golfer was fading fast,
His breathing was slow and weak.
He saw his foursome gathered round
And opened pale lips to speak.

"Be quiet and still!" the doctor said,
"You must save your energy!"
"*You* be quiet," the old man gasped,
"It is *my turn* on the tee!"

A sixty footer, lightly tapped, will roll right into the hole.

"Don't weep when I'm gone," he told them,
With a twinkle in his eye,
"I'm on my way at last to play
On that Golf Course in the Sky!"

"You play golf up there with angels,
Say, they are the nicest blokes:
When you putt they're Heavenly quiet
And they *never* count your strokes!

"The greens up there hold every shot,
Each putt takes a perfect roll.
A sixty-footer lightly tapped
Will roll straight into the hole!

"Sand traps up there are deep and wide,
But they *never* spoil your play,
If your shot should stray toward one
The sand trap just fades away!

"Tee shots up there fly straight and true,
Too far for the naked eye,
Then hit a rock and bounce again
On that Golf Course in the Sky!

"When your ball stops it's teed up nice
On clumps of grass or clover,
And if you have a hook or slice
The fairways just move over!

"The angels hover out of bounds
And if your shot shanks their way,
They meet the ball with flashing wings
To knock it back in play!

"You never wait to make a shot
Or let faster golfers by:
Each foursome has a private course
On that Golf Course in the Sky!

"The daylight lasts around the clock
And it goes without saying
A wink is all the sleep you need
You just keep right on playing!

"Don't weep for me," the old man smiled
  "For some day you too must go!
We'll play golf up there together
  If it's okay with the Pro!"

Then the golfer closed tired old eyes
  But he strained to speak once more.
To angels playing just ahead
  The old golfer whispered, "Fore!"

14

A GLOSSARY OF HELPFUL INFORMATION

AUTHOR'S NOTE: *My regular column, "What the !*!@!** is Bugging You Golfers?" draws many letters and questions. If you're still thinking about taking up the game, have taken it up, or are considering dropping it, some of these questions may be on the tip of your tongue. This, of course, may be your entire problem. Nobody can play golf with something on the tip of his tongue. But you may find the answer in these selected, profound, thoughtful and rewarding remarks I have passed along to troubled golfers.*

Q. How do you keep your wife from wanting to play golf with you?

A. Much of the delight of golf is due to the fact that wives stay home. If your wife wants to play with you, do not show resentment. Appear to welcome her warmly, but give her instruction. Do it every time she tees off with you. Keep this up long enough and she will lose all desire to be your golfing companion too.

Q. What should you wear when playing golf?

A. This depends a great deal where you're playing.

Even at the swankiest country clubs golfers lose their shirts every day, and nobody ostracizes them. The fabulous Stark Naked Country Club, located on the confines of one of the nation's largest nudist camps, requires no attire at all. Golfers wear their wallets scotch-taped to their hips. And when you get right down to it, a wallet is really the only essential accessory a golfer needs.

Q. What kind of shoes should I wear?

A. None, if you are playing golf at Stark Naked. On other courses, shoes with cleats are recommended. Never wear those jobs with ribbed soles. They tear up greens. And please, no tenny runners.

Q. In your columns you have frequently cautioned against riding in golf carts. What should I do if there is no way to get out of riding in a cart with a stranger?

A. You might try telling the driver that you get cart sick. Ask him to haul your clubs while you walk. If he *insists* that you ride in the cart with him you do have a problem, dearie. Anyway, sit erect and alert. Extend your left arm across the back of the seat and get a good grip. Keep both feet in the cart at all times. Watch the area ahead for holes, sprinkler heads, or petunias. Anticipate a sudden swerve. If at all possible, take tumbling lessons.

Q. When a stranger asks to join your threesome, how can you tell whether he is a fairly acceptable golfer or a rank beginner who will have you spend hours helping him hunt for balls?

A. When he offers to shake hands, extend your left. Explain that your right is sore. As you shake, feel his hand for calluses. If you feel none, remember a sudden telephone call you have to make and suggest that he join the group behind you. If he's wearing a golf glove and won't take it off so you can feel his calluses, give him the honor of teeing off first. If he seems undecided about which club to use off the first tee, get worried. If he finally selects a nine iron, you are in trouble. Head for that phone booth or better still, look for a Western Union Office.

Q. Many golfers buy new clubs every year. Are "model changes" really that significant in golf clubs?

A. Only if you manufacture clubs, or are a golfer who needs an alibi. What is really needed are new model golf balls. What the golf ball does is what causes all the frustration and tension. But manufacturers steadfastly refuse to change the design of golf balls. They remain monotonously round.

Q. I understand you should let faster golfers through. How do you do this tactfully?

A. Politely motion them through. Stand closely by as they hurry their shots. They usually goof and knock the ball in the woods. Then ask if you may play through while they hunt for their balls.

Q. What should you do if someone keeps driving into your foursome?

A. Walk back and get a good look at him. If he is bigger than you, compliment him on his drive. If he is smaller, ask him if he wants to play golf or fight.

Q. What should I do if I drive into another foursome?

A. Walk up to them politely and say, "I'm sorry, but I never dreamed I could hit one that far!" This is the accepted alibi.

Q. Is betting on golf permissible?

A. You are trying to pull my leg. I get enough letters from smart alecks as it is.

Q. What is a Robin?

A. There are two kinds. One is a bird. The other is a golf bet, but a bird helps here too. The players choose partners for three or six holes. Then they throw up and choose new partners.

Q. What is a Press Bet?

A. "Press" is short for pressure. When one golfer gets two or three holes ahead of the other, the loser frequently "Presses" or doubles the bet. This may be compounded into a press on a press pressing the pressed press.

Q. What is a Greenie?

A. A greenie is a tee shot that stops on the green and closest to the pin on a par three hole. The name is not derived from the putting green, as many think, but from the color of the other golfers' faces.

Q. What is a bingo, bango, bongo game?

A. This is a form of betting used only by golfers who, in working moments are bookkeepers, auditors, or C.P.A.'s. They give a point for the drive farthest off the tee and still in the fairway, a point for first on the green, a point for closest to the pin, a point for first in, a point for the low score on the hole, and a point to the guy with the sweetest breath.

Q. How can a beginner get other golfers to invite him to play with them?

A. First, practice hitting a ball and watching it roll to a stop. Be able to walk unerringly to it. When you learn to do this well, approach a threesome about to tee off and say, "Gentlemen, may I show you something?" Hit a ball out toward the nearest tall grass or trees. Watch it roll to a stop and then say, "Gentlemen, my ball has stopped by that small bush. I can walk unerringly to it. I always know where my ball stops rolling!" Then add, "I have never broken a hundred, but I do not believe in taking strokes." Pull out your wallet, extract a ten dollar bill, and say, "Can any of you gentlemen break a ten? I would like to buy the drinks for your fine threesome before you tee off with a vacancy." You will be invited to join them. No one minds playing with a beginner who always knows where his ball is, who is loose with money, has plenty of it, and who will bet without asking for strokes.

Q. How do you get a tee off time at a golf course?

A. Methods for arranging tee times vary with golf courses. Many municipal courses have a slanted pipe near the first tee in which each golfer drops a ball. As the first ball in line is removed, the others roll down into position and the owners tee off in that sequence. At these courses, find the boy who delivers the morning paper and tip him heavily to put your ball in the pipe well before dawn. Other clubs take telephone calls for tee-off times. They usually start taking the calls at 8 A.M. on Thursday for Saturday tee times. This is a tough one to beat. You can become President of the club, and thus get a choice tee time. Or talk to someone with the telephone company about methods of tying up the line so you'll be next. Some longtime dialers say you can dial all digits but the last one, hold it in the half-dialed position, and wait. This is supposed to tie up the line when the present conversation ends. After a time, release the dial and you're in. (Or still out, if it doesn't work.)

Many Clods use a simpler and more evil way to get

Some courses have no tee times or starter at the first tee.

a tee time. They wander by the golf course late in the week and sneak a look at Saturday reservations. Let's say they see a choice time reserved for Stan Slurch. They go home and have Mrs. Clod call the Pro shop. "Hello, Pro Shop," she says sweetly. "This is Mrs. Stan Slurch. Stan has been called out of town and asked me to cancel his tee time for Saturday morning." The Pro thanks her for this thoughtfulness and erases Stan. A few minutes later, Clod himself calls the shop and says, "Say, ol' buddy Pro, this is Claud Clod. I just found out I can play tomorrow. If you get any cancellations, would you put me down and call me?" And the Pro exclaims how he just had a cancellation and puts Claud down in Stan's place. Saturday morning Stan will be hard to handle and his wife will be in big trouble. Meanwhile Claud Clod and his friends are hacking merrily along.

Q. Some courses have no tee times and no starter at the first tee. How can you tell who is up next and how can you courteously tee off at these places?

A. You can't. There is no courteous way. Just charge up to the tee and yell, "Who's off next?" This may start a fight. If it does, slip out of the scuffling and tee off. At some courses, where meek little guys play, you can just push right up as though you had a tee time and tee off. As the last guy in a foursome hits, step forward and say, "Well, gang, it's eight fifteen and that's us!" Tee up your ball and fire away. At one course, golfers used a slant pipe and the rolling line of balls to regulate teeing off sequence. They conformed, but each Saturday morning, at exactly eight o'clock, a lone little old lady showed up dragging a golf cart. She paid no attention to the huge gathering of waiting golfers or the balls in the slant pipe but strode to the tee. She teed up her ball, waited until the foursome ahead was out of range, whacked the ball, and headed off down the fairway. This went on Saturday after Saturday with no one daring to accost the little old lady. I still have the wig and granny dress, in case you'd like to borrow it some Saturday.

15

MOMENT OF DECISION

NOW THAT WE'VE COVERED THE REALLY IMPORTANT THINGS you should consider before taking up golf, the time has come for you to make a decision. Will you continue to putter around the yard each Saturday in the stiff, sweaty clothes you hung up last weekend? Will you flop in an easy chair for an entire afternoon watching the idiot box? Or will you, knowing all that lurks in store for you on the golf course, cast logic to the winds and join our hacking, sweating, frustrated but delighted horde?

Come and join us. You can play now and swing later. Any threesome on any course will be glad to have you for a fourth if you show them your backswing and wallet. And if you don't find a threesome with an opening, we'd be delighted to have you join ours. We have an opening because one guy in our group has been winning far too often. I would like to remind you before we make our bets that I have been working on this book for a couple of months and with no action my game has gone to pot. Of course you'll have to give me strokes, but it will be mighty nice having you and your wallet with us in this delightful game called golf.

Come and join our hacking, sweating, frustrated but delighted horde!

16

LAST LINES

IF YOU GOT BACK TO HERE AND STILL FEEL YOU DIDN'T GET your money's worth, we have stuck a couple of special little gems here to amuse you. This also gives us more time to get to the bank with your money.

Send a cheerful "Get Well" card
To "No Teeth" Finney
He drove into a foursome,
One time too many!

* * *

It's for Golfer Dan
The bell is tolling
He picked up a ball
That was still rolling.

* * *

LAST MAN'S LAMENT

I always tee off last
'Cause my backswing's so fast!

And we'd like to leave you with one last pleasant thought. This book contains 89 pages. If you used no more than that to get to here, you parred it. Congratulations!